HOW TO START & SCALE AN AIRBNB BUSINESS

Beginners Guide to Marketing Your Listings, Quit Your Day Job and Earn Full-time Income

Ricardo B. Salls

CONTENTS

INTRODUCTIONS _____5

CHAPTER ONE _____7

  MARKET RESEARCH AND PLANNING _____7

    1 relating Your Target followership _____7

    2 assaying Original Regulations and Zoning Laws _____7

    3 Assessing Competition in Your Area _____7

    4 Request trends and openings _____8

    5 Threat Analysis and Contingency Planning _____8

    6 Sustainable Practices _____8

    7 Financial protrusions and Budgeting _____9

    8 Technology and Innovation _____9

    9 Social and Cultural Sensitivity _____9

    10 Marketing Strategy Alignment_____9

CHAPTER TWO _____11

  PROPERTY PREPARATION AND STYLING _____11

    Creating a Drinking Atmosphere _____11

    Essential Amenities and Features_____11

    Budget-Friendly Interior Design Tips _____12

    Safety and Security Measures_____13

    drawing and conservation Protocols _____13

    Photography and Virtual tenures _____14

    Guest primers and Information _____14

CHAPTER THREE _____17

  LEGAL AND FINANCIAL CONSIDERATIONS _____17

    Tax Implications and Record-Keeping_____17

    Insurance for Airbnb Hosts _____21

    Lease Agreements and Contracts _____25

CHAPTER FOUR_____29

  SETTING UP YOUR AIRBNB LISTING _____29

    Writing an Attractive Property Description _____29

Pricing Strategies and Dynamic Pricing Tools_____34

*CHAPTER FIVE*_____**39**

OPTIMIZING YOUR AIRBNB PROFILE _____**39**
Start with a Top position_____39
The impact of this strategy on your rankings can be instant. _____44

*CHAPTER SIX*_____**49**

MARKETING YOUR AIRBNB BUSINESS _____**49**
How do I advertise my Airbnb on social media? _____49
Collaborating with Local Businesses for Airbnb Success _____53

*CHAPTER SEVEN*_____**59**

SCALING YOUR AIRBNB BUSINESS _____**59**
how to Expand Your Property Portfolio on Airbnb_____59
Hiring Assistance and Outsourcing Tasks for Airbnb Success _____64

*CHAPTER EIGHT*_____**71**

CASE STUDIES AND SUCCESS STORIES ON AIRBNB _____**71**
Unveiling the Secrets of Airbnb Triumph _____71

*CHAPTER NINE*_____**75**

THE RESOURCES AND TOOLS FOR AIRBNB HOSTS _____**75**
Elevate Your Airbnb Hosting Game _____75

*CONCLUSION*_____**81**

MASTERING THE ART OF AIRBNB BUSINESS _____**81**

INTRODUCTIONS

In the ever-evolving geography of ultramodern trips and accommodation, the Airbnb platform has surfaced as a revolutionary force, reshaping the way individuals experience and engage with their peregrinations. As we step into the dynamic realm of Airbnb hosting, we embark on a trip that goes further than simply furnishing lodging; it's about creating unique, substantiated guests that leave an unforgettable mark on the rubberneck's memory.

The Airbnb business model has transcended traditional hospitality, allowing individuals to open their doors and spaces to a global community seeking further than just a place to stay. Whether you are a homeowner with a spare room, an audacious entrepreneur looking to invest in parcels, or someone eager to transfigure their living space into a haven for trippers, the openings within the Airbnb sphere are bottomless.

This companion is drafted to be your compass in navigating the complications of the Airbnb geography in(Current Time). From understanding request trends and legal considerations to curating indelible guest gests, we claw into the strategies and perceptivity that can elevate your hosting trip to new heights. As the participating frugality continues to thrive, embracing the Airbnb business presents a chance not only to induce income but also to become a vital part of a global community that values connection, artistic exchange, and a sense of belonging.

So, whether you are a seasoned host looking to upgrade your approach or a freshman seeking to embark on this instigative adventure, join us as we unleash the secrets to a successful Airbnb business. Your adventure in the world of hospitality begins then, where the possibilities are as different as the guests who'll soon call your space home.

CHAPTER ONE
MARKET RESEARCH AND PLANNING

1 relating Your Target followership

- Demographic Analysis
- Understanding the age, gender, occupation, and interests of your implicit guests.
- Segmentation Strategy
- Creating client parts grounded on trip purposes (business, rest, family recesses) to knitter your immolations.

2 assaying Original Regulations and Zoning Laws

- Legal Landscape
- probing original and public regulations affecting short-term settlements.
- relating zoning laws and restrictions on property use in your area.
- Permitting Process
- Understanding the process of carrying permits and licenses for Airbnb hosting.

3 Assessing Competition in Your Area

- Contender Analysis
- assessing other Airbnb rosters in your vicinity.
- relating unique selling points and implicit gaps in the request.
- Price Benchmarking

- assaying pricing strategies of challengers to determine competitive rates.

4 Request trends and openings

- Industry Trends
- Staying informed about the recent trends in the short-term reimbursement assiduity.
- relating arising hospitality trends that could impact your business.
- Seasonal Demand
- assaying seasonal oscillations in demand and conforming your strategy consequently.

5 Threat Analysis and Contingency Planning

- Risk Assessment
- relating implicit pitfalls similar to natural disasters, profitable downturns, or global events.
- Developing contingency plans to alleviate pitfalls and ensure business durability.
- Security Measures
- enforcing security measures for both guests and property.

6 Sustainable Practices

- Environmental Impact
- Assessing the environmental impact of your Airbnb business.
- Incorporating sustainable practices and promoting eco-friendly enterprise.

7 Financial protrusions and Budgeting

- Financial Modeling
- Creating realistic profit and expenditure protrusions for your Airbnb business.
- Developing a budget that includes original setup costs, ongoing charges, and implicit extremities.

8 Technology and Innovation

- Smart Technologies
- Exploring technology results in enhancing the guest experience (crucial entry, smart home features).
- Staying streamlined on innovative tools and platforms for Airbnb hosts.

9 Social and Cultural Sensitivity

- Cultural Considerations
- Understanding and esteeming artistic nuances that may impact guest relations.
- Promoting diversity and inclusivity in your Airbnb business.

10 Marketing Strategy Alignment

- Aligning with Branding
- icing your marketing strategy aligns with the brand image you want to convey.
- exercising marketing channels that reverberate with your target followership.

This chapter provides a comprehensive companion to conducting request exploration and planning for your Airbnb business. By understanding your followership, legal geography, competition, and assiduity trends, you can develop a solid foundation for a successful adventure.

CHAPTER TWO
PROPERTY PREPARATION AND STYLING
Creating a Drinking Atmosphere

- **Interior Design Aesthetics**

- opting for a cohesive theme or style that aligns with the target followership.
- Incorporating rudiments that elicit a warm and inviting air.
- **Comfortable Furnishings**

- Choosing comfortable and durable cabinetwork for an affable guest experience.
- Optimizing seating arrangements and bedroom layouts for functionality.
- **particular Touches**

- Adding substantiated scenery particulars to produce a unique and memorable space.
- Incorporating original rudiments or themes that reflect the property's surroundings.

Essential Amenities and Features

- **Functional Kitchen and Dining Areas**

- Equipping the kitchen with essential appliances and implements.
- Creating a comfortable dining space for guests to enjoy reflections.
- **High- Quality Coverlet and Linens**

- Investing in comfortable mattresses and ultra-expensive quality bed linens.
- furnishing redundant pillows and robes for a luxurious sense.
- **Modern Technology Integration**

- Installing smart home features for convenience (smart cinches, thermostats, lighting).
- Offering high-speed internet and entertainment options for tech-smart guests.

Budget-Friendly Interior Design Tips

- **DIY Decor results**

- enforcing cost-effective do-it-yourself scenery systems.
- exercising online coffers for budget-friendly interior design alleviation.
- **Multi-Functional Furniture**
- Opting for cabinetwork that serves multiple purposes, maximizing space.

- Incorporating the storehouse results in decluttering and organizing the space.
- **Thrifty Yet Stylish Decor**

- Combing providence stores and online commerce for unique and affordable scenery particulars.
- Repurposing includes cabinetwork and accessories for a sustainable and budget-friendly approach.

Safety and Security Measures

- **exigency Preparedness**

- furnishing exigency information and procedures for guests.
- Installing bank sensors, fire extinguishers, and first aid accouterments.
- **Secure Entry Systems**

- icing the safety of guests with secure entry systems.
- enforcing crucial entry options for added convenience.

drawing and conservation Protocols

- **Thorough Cleaning Procedures**
- Establishing a cleaning schedule to maintain a pristine terrain.

- Employing professional cleaning services to ensure high norms.
- **Regular conservation Checks**

- Conducting routine examinations for wear and tear and gash.
- Addressing conservation issues instantly to enhance guest satisfaction.

Photography and Virtual tenures

- **Professional Photography**

- Hiring a professional shooter to capture the property's stylish features.
- Showcasing the space in different lighting conditions and angles.
- **Virtual tenures**

- Creating virtual tenures to give a comprehensive view of the property.
- pressing unique features and dealing points through interactive media.

Guest primers and Information

- **Comprehensive Guest primers**

- collecting detailed primers with essential information about the property and original area.
- Including instructions for using appliances, exigency procedures, and original recommendations.
- **Original Area Guide**

- furnishing guests with a curated companion to nearby lodestones, cafes, and services.
- uniting with original businesses for special offers or hookups.

This chapter attendants hosts through the process of preparing and baptizing their Airbnb property. By fastening on creating a welcoming atmosphere, incorporating essential amenities, enforcing budget-friendly design tips, and prioritizing safety, hosts can enhance the overall guest experience and separate their tables in a competitive request.

CHAPTER THREE
LEGAL AND FINANCIAL CONSIDERATIONS
Tax Implications and Record-Keeping

Understanding Duty Scores

- duty Bracket
- Determining the applicable duty bracket for your Airbnb business (sole procurement, LLC, pot).
- Consulting with a duty professional to ensure compliance with original and public duty laws.
- Income duty Considerations
- Reporting rental income directly on particular or business duty returns.
- relating deductible charges to optimize duty liability.

Deductible Charges for Airbnb Hosts

- Property-Affiliated Deductions
- Abating mortgage interest, property levies, and deprecation.
- establishing home advancements and repairs that qualify for deductions.
- Operating Charges
- Tracking and abating charges related to property conservation, serviceability, and inventories.
- Including costs associated with marketing, cleaning, and guest amenities.

Deals and residency levies

- Deals duty Compliance
- Understanding the connection of deals duty on short-term settlements in your governance.
- Registering for and remitting deals duty to the applicable authorities.
- **residency duty Compliance**
- probing original regulations regarding residency levies.
- icing accurate collection and remittance of residency levies from guests.

Record- Keeping Stylish Practices

- **Organized Financial Records**
- Establishing a methodical system for organizing fiscal documents.
- exercising account software to track income, charges, and bills.
- **Guest Records**
- Maintaining detailed records of guest stays, including check- heft and check-out dates.
- establishing any issues or judgments related to guest relations.

Quarterly and Year-End Reporting

- **Quarterly Tax Filings**
- clinging to daily duty from conditions to avoid penalties.
- Reviewing fiscal records regularly to ensure delicacy.
- **Time-End Reporting**
- Preparing for time-end duty reporting, including the allocation of 1099 forms to service providers.

- Conducting a comprehensive fiscal review to identify implicit deductions.

Engaging Professional Assistance

- **Tax Advisor Consultation**
- Seeking guidance from a duty professional with experience in short-term settlements.
- Agitating duty planning strategies to optimize fiscal issues.
- **Legal Counsel**
- Consulting with legal professionals to ensure compliance with ever-changing duty laws.
- Addressing any legal enterprises related to the operation of an Airbnb business.

International Tax Considerations

- **Cross-Border duty Counteraccusations**
- Understanding duty scores for hosts operating in multiple authorities.
- Complying with transnational duty laws and covenants.

Staying Informed About Duty Changes Nonstop Learning

- Staying informed about updates and changes in duty laws affecting short-term settlements.
- Subscribing to assiduity publications and attending applicable shops or webinars.

This chapter provides hosts with a comprehensive understanding of the duty counteraccusations associated with running an Airbnb business. By maintaining accurate records, understanding deductible charges, and seeking professional advice, hosts can navigate the complex geography of duty scores and optimize their fiscal issues.

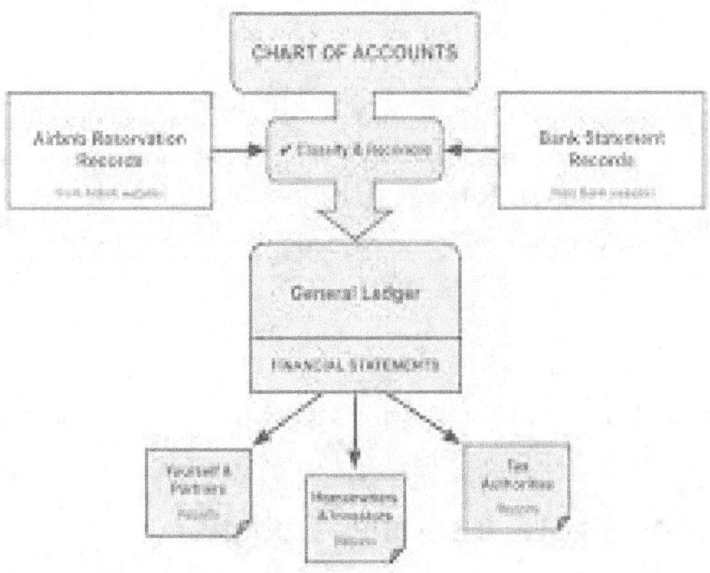

Understanding Airbnb Host Protection

- Host Guarantee. Host Protection Insurance

- secerns between Airbnb's Host Guarantee, which covers property damage, and Host Protection Insurance, which provides liability content.
- **Coverage Limits and Rejections**

- Exploring the compass and limitations of Airbnb's insurance immolations.
- Understanding specific scripts that may not be covered by Airbnb's programs.

Supplemental Insurance Options

- **Short- Term -Short-reimbursement insurance programs**

- probing and opting for supplemental insurance programs acclimatized for short-term settlements.
- Assessing content for property damage, liability, and loss of income.
- **marketable Liability Insurance**

- Exploring marketable liability insurance options for fresh protection.

- assessing programs that cover fleshly injury, property damage, and legal charges.

Property and Contents Insurance

- **Specialized Airbnb Coverage**

- relating insurance providers that offer technical content for Airbnb hosts.
- icing content for structural damage, theft, and vandalization.
- **Valuables and particular things**

- Understanding content for particular things inside the property.
- Encouraging guests to gain their trip insurance for particular particulars.

Guest Vetting and threat operation

- **Webbing Guests**

- enforcing a guest webbing process to reduce the threat of property damage or liability issues.
- Communicating house rules and prospects to guests before their stay.
- **Security Measures**
- Installing security features, similar to surveillance cameras and secure entry systems.

- Notifying guests about security measures in place to enhance safety.

Deductibles and Claims Process

- **Insurance Deductibles**

- Understanding the deductible quantities associated with insurance programs.
- assessing the impact of deductibles on the overall cost and content.
- **Effective Claims Process**

- Familiarize yourself with the claims process for each insurance policy.
- Keeping detailed records and attestation in case of a claim.

exigency Preparedness

- **exigency Connections and Procedures**

- furnishing guests with exigency contact information.
- Establishing clear procedures for extremities, including evacuation plans.
- **Crisis Communication Plan**
- Developing a communication plan to address guests and authorities during heads.
- Keeping a list of near medical installations and exigency services.

Regular Insurance Policy Reviews

- **Policy Updates and Renewals**
- Regularly reviewing insurance programs to ensure they align with current requirements.
- streamlining content as the property evolves or regulations change.

Legal Consultation

- **Legal Advice for Insurance Matters**
- Seeking legal counsel to understand the legal counteraccusations of insurance opinions.
- Addressing any legal enterprises related to liability and insurance content.

This chapter equips Airbnb hosts with the knowledge and tools demanded to navigate the complex geography of insurance. By understanding Airbnb's immolations, exploring supplemental insurance options, and enforcing threat operation strategies, hosts can cover their property, means, and guests effectively.

Customizing Lease Agreements

- o Tailoring Agreements to Your Property

- o Creating parcel agreements that reflect the unique features and rules of your Airbnb property.
- o easily outlining property-specific details, similar to check-heft/ eschewal times and house rules.
- o **Legal Review**

- o Seeking legal advice to ensure parcel agreements misbehave with original regulations.
- o Addressing common legal considerations, similar to liability and remuneration clauses.

Guest prospects and House Rules

- o **Setting Clear prospects**
- o easily communicating guest liabilities and prospects during their stay.
- o Outlining house rules regarding noise situations, smoking, and other property-specific guidelines.
- o **Customizing for Each Stay**
- o acclimatizing house rules grounded on the nature of the guest's stay(e.g., family holiday, business trip).
- o easily stating consequences for violating house rules.

Payment and Cancellation Terms

- Payment Details
- Specifying payment terms, including deposit conditions and accepted payment styles.
- easily communicating the total cost of the stay, including any fresh freights.
- Cancellation programs

- Defining cancellation programs to manage guest prospects.
- Offering inflexibility options while guarding the host's fiscal interests.

Duration of Stay and Renewal Terms

- Defining Reimbursement Ages

- easily stating the duration of the guest's stay.
- Outlining renewal options for longer-term guests and the process for extending stays.
- Check-in and Check-out Procedures

- Detailing check-heft and check-out procedures to ensure a smooth transition between guests.
- furnishing instructions for returning keys or access bias.

Property Conservation and Care

- Guest liabilities
- Outlining guest liabilities for maintaining the property during their stay.

- o Setting prospects for cleanliness and reporting any damages instantly.
- o **Host liabilities**
- o easily stating the host's liabilities for property and repairs.
- o Establishing procedures for addressing conservation issues during a guest's stay.

Confidentiality and sequestration

- o **programs**
- o Addressing sequestration enterprises and outlining the host's commitment to guest sequestration.
- o Setting prospects for any surveillance or monitoring bias on the property.
- o **Confidentiality Clauses**
- o Including confidentiality clauses to cover sensitive information.
- o easily stating the running of guest data in compliance with sequestration laws.

Force Majeure and Contingency Clauses

- o **Force Majeure Events**
- o Defining force majeure events that may impact the guest's stay.
- o Establishing procedures for handling cancellations or changes due to unlooked-for circumstances.
- o **Contingency Planning**
- o Including contingency clauses to address unanticipated issues similar to property damage or natural disasters.
- o Outlining procedures for shifting guests in case of extremities.

Legal Compliance and Original Regulations

- o Regulatory Compliance
- o Ensuring parcel agreements cleave to original regulations and zoning laws.
- o Staying informed about changes in original legislation that may affect the terms of the agreement.

establishing Communication

- o Written Communication
- o Encouraging written communication to produce a record of relations.
- o establishing important exchanges or agreements via dispatch or messaging platforms.

Professional Review and Updates

- o Regular Legal Review
- o Periodically seeking legal review to modernize parcel agreements grounded on changing regulations.
- o icing agreements remain fairly sound and applicable.

This chapter provides Airbnb hosts with a comprehensive companion to creating effective parcel agreements and contracts. By customizing agreements, setting clear prospects, and addressing legal considerations, hosts can establish a frame that protects both their property and the guest experience. Regular reviews and updates ensure that agreements remain applicable and fairly biddable over time.

CHAPTER FOUR
SETTING UP YOUR AIRBNB LISTING
Writing an Attractive Property Description

Casting a Compelling Preface

witching Opening

- Creating an attention-grabbing preface that highlights the unique features of your property.
- Using descriptive language to elicit a sense of excitement and expectation.

Setting the Scene

- oil a pictorial picture of the property's surroundings and the experience it offers.
- Incorporating original lodestones, milestones, and amenities.

pressing crucial Features and Amenities

point- concentrated Descriptions

- easily outlining the name features that make your property special.
- Emphasizing amenities similar to a pool, private theater, or panoramic views.

Comfort and Convenience

- Describing the comfort-enhancing rudiments, similar to decoration coverlets, ultramodern appliances, and thoughtful design.
- Emphasizing convenience factors like propinquity to public transportation or popular lodestones.

Tailoring to Your Target Followership

Understanding Your Guests

- relating the target followership for your property (e.g., families, business trippers, adventure campaigners).
- acclimatizing the description to punctuate aspects that appeal specifically to your target demographic.

Addressing Guest Needs

- Anticipating and addressing implicit guest needs in the property description.
- Emphasizing features that feed to the preferences of your ideal guests.

Creating an Engaging Story

Narrative Approach

- Weaving a narrative that tells the story of the guest's experience during their stay.
- Creating a sense of emotional connection and absorption.

Descriptive Language

- Using suggestive and sensitive language to engage the anthology's imagination.
- Inviting guests to fantasize about themselves enjoying the space.

furnishing Practical Information

Logistical Details

- Including practical details similar to the number of bedrooms, restroom configurations, and sleeping arrangements.
- Clarifying any unique aspects of the property layout.

Availability and Safety

- pressing availability features and safety measures in place.
- furnishing information about near medical installations and exigency services.

Showcasing Original gests

Original Recommendations

- Incorporating recommendations for near caffs, lodestones, and conditioning.
- Showcasing the property's connection to the original culture and community.

Unique Selling Points

- relating and emphasizing the unique selling points of the original area.
- secerns your property by showcasing what makes it a gateway to a unique trip experience.

eliciting Emotion with Imagery

High- Quality prints

- icing that property prints are high-resolution and showcase the space directly.
- Using a variety of images to punctuate different aspects of the property.

Virtual tenures

- Mentioning the vacuity of virtual tenures to give an immersive exercise for implicit guests.
- Encouraging guests to explore the property nearly before making a booking.

Encouraging Interaction and Bookings

Call to Action

- Including a clear call to action that encourages guests to bespeak or interrogate.
- Creating a sense of urgency or exclusivity to prompt hastily opinions.

Transparent Communication

- Setting clear prospects about what guests can anticipate during their stay.
- Encouraging open communication and responsiveness.

Guest Witnesses and Reviews

Incorporating Positive Feedback

- Integrating positive guest witnesses and reviews into the property description.
- pressing specific aspects that former guests have praised.

nonstop Optimization

Feedback Analysis

- Regularly reviewing guest feedback to identify areas for enhancement.
- streamlining the property description grounded on guest suggestions and changing request trends.

Staying Competitive

- Monitoring challengers' rosters and conforming to your property description to stay competitive.
- Keeping the description fresh with updates and seasonal highlights.

This chapter provides hosts with a comprehensive companion to casting a seductive property description on Airbnb. By combining engaging liars, practical information, and a focus on the property's unique features, hosts can produce a compelling narrative that entices implicit guests and sets their table piecemeal in a competitive request. nonstop optimization grounded on guest feedback ensures that the property description remains applicable and charming over time.

Understanding Pricing Dynamics

Market Research

- Conducting thorough request exploration to understand pricing trends in your area.
- assaying the rates of similar parcels to set a competitive yet profitable pricing strategy.

Seasonal oscillations

- Feting the impact of seasonal demand on pricing.
- conforming rates to align with peak and off-peak ages.

Establishing Base Rates

Cost Analysis

- Conducting a comprehensive cost analysis, including property conservation, serviceability, and functional charges.
- Setting a base rate that ensures profitability while remaining seductive to implicit guests.

Competitive Pricing

- Balancing competitive pricing with the unique value propositions of your property.
- Offering promotional rates or abatements for longer stays to attract different guest parts.

Dynamic Pricing Principles

Real-Time Demand Analysis

- exercising dynamic pricing tools to dissect real-time demand for your property.
- conforming rates grounded on factors similar to original events, leaves, and request demand.

contender Pricing Monitoring

- Keeping a close eye on contender pricing and conforming your rates consequently.
- enforcing strategies to separate your property and justify decoration pricing.

Guest geste and Booking Patterns

Booking Window Considerations

- assaying guest booking patterns, including lead times and last-nanosecond bookings.
- conforming pricing to incentivize early bookings or subsidize short-notice stays.

Length-of-Stay Abatements

- Offering abatements for longer stays to attract guests looking for extended accommodation.
- enforcing tiered pricing structures for different lengths of stay.

Special Events and leaves

Event Pricing Strategies

- conforming rates for special events, carnivals, or peak tourism seasons.

- using dynamic pricing tools to subsidize increased demand during specific ages.

Holiday Pricing

- enforcing vacation-specific pricing strategies.
- Offering elevations or package deals to attract guests during gleeful seasons.

Dynamic Pricing Tools and Platforms

Third-Party Tools

- Exploring third-party dynamic pricing tools that integrate with Airbnb.
- Assessing features similar to robotization, real-time request data, and contender analysis.

Airbnb Smart Pricing

- using Airbnb's Smart Pricing point to automate pricing adaptations.
- Fine-tuning settings to align with your specific pricing strategy.

Data Analysis and Adjustment Frequency

Regular Data Reviews

- Establishing a routine for reviewing pricing data and performance criteria.
- conforming pricing strategies grounded on the effectiveness of former changes.

Seasonal adaptations

- enforcing seasonal adaptations in advance to stay ahead of request trends.
- Planning for special elevations or abatements during specific seasons.

Guest fidelity and reprise Business

fidelity Programs

- enforcing fidelity programs to encourage reprise bookings.
- Offering special rates or gratuities for guests who have stayed at your property multiple times.

Promotional juggernauts

- Running targeted promotional juggernauts for one guest.
- Using dynamic pricing tools to knitter offers grounded on guest history and preferences.

Monitoring and conforming to Guest Feedback

Feedback Analysis

- assaying guest feedback related to pricing.
- conforming pricing strategies grounded on guest suggestions and comprehension of value.

nonstop literacy and adaption

Staying Informed

- Keeping abreast of assiduity trends and changes in the original request.
- Continuously learning from data analysis and conforming strategies consequently.

Experimentation and Innovation

- Experimenting with different pricing models and strategies.
- Embracing invention in dynamic pricing tools and technologies.

This chapter provides hosts with a comprehensive companion to developing effective pricing strategies and exercising dynamic pricing tools on Airbnb. By understanding request dynamics, enforcing real-time adaptations, and using data-driven perceptivity, hosts can optimize their pricing strategies to attract guests, maximize profit, and stay competitive in the dynamic short-term reimbursement request.

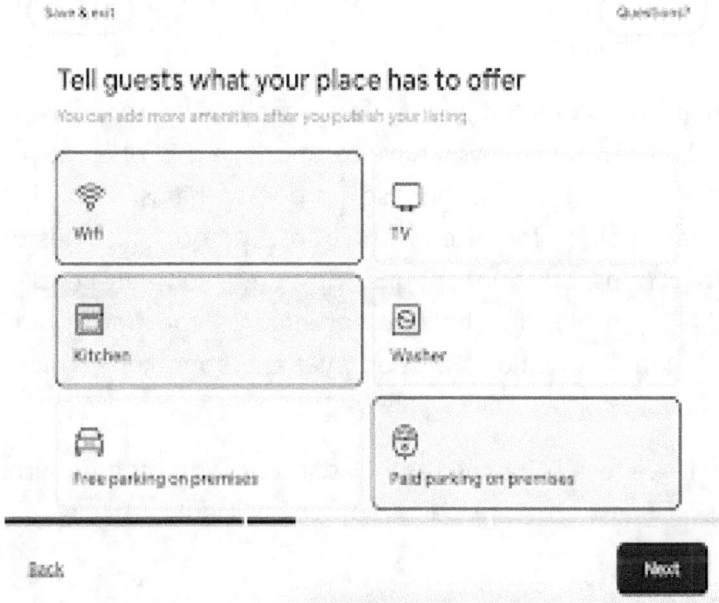

CHAPTER FIVE
OPTIMIZING YOUR AIRBNB PROFILE

As a host, there are lots of effects that you can do to get your table to rank advanced on Airbnb hunt results, both during setup and later. Then are some tips on how to boost Airbnb

Start with a Top position

Airbnb itself says that the position of a property plays a major part in its position in hunt results. Preference is given to places that are close to popular sightseer lodestones that guests like to visit during their stays in the area.

position isn't a commodity you can change just to please the Airbnb SEO algorithm, so you have to prioritize this when buying a short-term reimbursement. Choose a property that isn't only in the stylish metropolises for Airbnb but also near original lodestones and public transportation options. However, you can check out Awning's Top Deals for holiday settlements for trade in high locales, If you don't enjoy a property yet and don't know where to start.

still, you'll see results incontinently, as soon as you list it on Airbnb, If you choose a strategic place for your investment.

Offer Competitive Amenities: Airbnb also suggests that hosts should strive for fashion ability among guests to rank advanced, and one way to do that is to offer amenities that are in high demand and low force. It's each about outperforming the competition.

For major effects like swimming pools, hot barrels, and out-of-door quadrangles, you'd need to plan and search for a property that has these features before buying, or at least the space. For simpler effects like a restroom, air-exertion, high-speed internet, streaming services, and grills, you can search what hard-listed parcels are offering and try to eclipse them. In utmost cases, investing in many largely demanded amenities will more than pay for itself by boosting the ranking of your Airbnb and getting you further bookings and therefore further income.

While you can enter amenities during the table process, you can always go back and add further as they become available. The further amenity boxes you can check on your table, the better for Airbnb SEO and residency, but make sure you don't exaggerate as this will hurt you. As you make plutocrat from your Airbnb business, it's worth adding a new amenity in a while, especially as competition increases in the area.

Complete Your Profile and Update Your Listing

You need to work on Airbnb SEO as soon as you get on the platform. When first subscribing as a host, make sure that you fill in your profile in full with all details. Airbnb and guests likewise value translucency. The same holds for your table-complete all available information. Don't spare your sweats when listing on Airbnb because it'll award you as soon as your table goes live.

While the bulk of the work has to be done when you first get started, this isn't a one-time thing. You need to modernize your table regularly whenever you change anything around or when you notice a change in demand among guests or a change in force among hosts. perhaps you started offering an experience, or perhaps you forgot to mention an amenity or an original magnet when you created your table. It's no way too late to optimize.

As a rule of thumb, try to modernize your table at least once a month to show the Airbnb algorithm that you're staying up to date. Results should be immediate as Airbnb aims to give up-to-date rosters to guests first.

Use Professional prints

One of the pillars of Airbnb SEO is furnishing a quality table, and a crucial point of a high-quality table is the prints. Airbnb won't let you upload photos below a certain size as they want Filmland to be high quality, high resolution, and rather professional. They should cover all apartments and spaces, present different angles, and punctuate the amenities that your property provides. That's a straightforward way to show implicit guests that your reimbursement is better than others in the area and to get them to bespeak with you.

still, Airbnb offers professional photography in some requests, If you're reluctant to coordinate the process yourself. Top Airbnb operation companies can cover this service too.

Upload professional prints as soon as you produce your Airbnb listing to optimize for the underpinning algorithm. Whenever you redecorate the property, refurnish it, or apply major repairs, flashback to change the prints with a new high-quality batch. It's pivotal that you punctuate the cons of your property and that the reimbursement matches the listing exactly (to avoid negative commentary which will hurt your ranking).

Optimize Your Airbnb Title and Prioritize for Hunt

Another thing you can do in your table title to boost Airbnb SEO is to punctuate milestones. You shouldn't only buy a property in a top position for Airbnb but also show the Airbnb algorithm and guests that your reimbursement offers high access to sightseer lodestones. For this case, you can write a commodity like "Experience the Majesty of the Grand Canyon'' rather than writing " Stay in Sedona ". Meanwhile, flashback to keep symbols and emojis out of your Airbnb titles. That's against Airbnb's content policy.

Anything you do with the title of your table should have an immediate impact. However, keep experimenting until you get it right, If the results aren't positive. However, half-service Airbnb operation results like Red Awning and Evolve offer listing optimization through SEO and content, If you need help. But keep in mind, you'll still need to handle the drawing yourself, and at 10 of the profit it might be worth getting a full-service property director.

Make Sure Your Description Is Scannable

Organize your table description in a way that makes it easy for hosts to just overlook it rather than having to read every single detail. You have only 500 characters to optimize this both for Airbnb SEO and guests. Break down the description into short sections with headlines in bold, each of which highlights one crucial point of your property. Use pellet points and numbered lists. This will allow guests to get all the important words snappily, without getting lost in gratuitous details. You don't have to use up all the space.

Try to make this scannable from the progeny go, but don't worry if it doesn't produce optimal results. You can always go back and paraphrase your description to see if this will boost bookings and residency. Other than that, make sure you modernize your description every time there's a significant change in your property. This is a commodity you should readdress regularly, conforming for the season, any major events in the area, or simply to ameliorate the table.

produce a Guidebook to Include in Your Listing

Another way to ameliorate Airbnb SEO is to add a guidebook to your table. The platform has a devoted point, where you can give particular recommendations to unborn guests on how to make the most out of your property or how to enjoy the area. You can include lists of top lodestones and your particular pets and must-dos. Airbnb reports increased reserving rates among rosters with guidebooks. Flashback that it's each about serving guests and their requirements.

You can start with a simple guidebook and add to it over time, especially if you're a remote investor who's not too familiar with the original request and original lodestones. It's still worth adding some content to the guidebook as soon as you list to get this immediate boost.

Set Up Competitive Pricing

Airbnb itself considers pricing as one of the three most important factors for its ranking algorithm. From an Airbnb SEO point of view, the pricing of your table shouldn't exceed the prevailing nocturnal rates for similar parcels with analogous amenities in the area. Indeed, Airbnb will propose a reasonable diurnal rate for your property type and request, grounded on giveaways. One way you can push up your rate without hurting your ranking is by adding further amenities to your reimbursement to outperform the competition.

So that your profit doesn't suffer from lowering your nocturnal rates, apply dynamic pricing, which means changing rates depending on seasonality, and weekdays. weekends, public leaves, and original demand and force. Airbnb offers this option through Smart Pricing, which will automatically acclimate your rates daily to accommodate changes in demand and force. Alternatively, you can also use third-party tools like Air DNA Smart Rates, Beyond Pricing, and Price Labs.

The impact of this strategy on your rankings can be instant.

Keep Your Booking Timetable Up to Date

There are two main affects you can do to optimize your timetable. First, maximize your vacuity window, i.e., keep your timetable open for numerous months in advance so that guests can formerly bespeak their holiday a time from now. Second, if you plan to use your property for particular reasons, block the timetable well in advance. You want to have your timetable up to date at all times. The further vacuity your table has, the more likely it's to show up in a hunt covering any unborn time.

In case you list on other platforms too, Airbnb provides you with the option to import timetables. robotization tools similar to Evolve and Guest allow you to sync timetables too.

Lower the minimal Length of Stay

Airbnb allows you to set up a minimal stay for trip length in case you'd like to feed longer-term guests. Still, this goes against stylish practices for Airbnb SEO. After all, you want your table to apply to as numerous quests as possible. However, you'll automatically push down all guests looking for 1- or 2- 2-night stays, hurting your residency and your ranking, If you have a minimal stay demand. It's stylish to have a minimal stay of 1 night (the dereliction).

This tactic can work incontinently as your property will start popping up in the quests of short-length stays right down.

Promote Your Property Outside Airbnb

You shouldn't limit your Airbnb SEO sweats to the platform itself. You should promote your table on other digital channels including your holiday rental website (you should have one), emails you shoot out to your network, host communities and forums, etc. The further business you bring to your table (indeed from external sources), the further bookings you might get, which will boost your ranking in the future.

You need to work on marketing and promoting your property outside Airbnb for maximum results. However, for illustration, for dispatch marketing, If you have access to any marketing robotization tools.

make a Social Media runner for Your Listing

Another external strategy is to produce a social media runner for your table where you add prints and a description and also link directly to the table on Airbnb. The further views you get, the more likely someone is to bespeak.

erecting a social media runner shouldn't take important of your time, but you should continue streamlining it and posting on it on a daily base(at least) to optimize engagement. This is a good place to talk about original events and lodestones to get more people to visit the area and stay at your property.

Test Paid Advertising

Last but not least, you can try running Google Advertisements or Facebook Advertisements on your table. This will surely bring a lot of good business to your Airbnb table, with all the benefits that this generates. still, the cost of advertisements can be too high to achieve a good overall ROI.

We'd recommend that you start with a small budget while the advertisement algorithms learn about your stylish target followership and start optimizing performance. In many weeks, you can estimate whether advertisements are helping your table rank advanced on Airbnb or not. In this way, you don't threaten losing plutocrat from promoting your table, rather than making plutocrat

CHAPTER SIX

MARKETING YOUR AIRBNB BUSINESS

How do I advertise my Airbnb on social media?

Advertising your Airbnb on social media involves a strategic approach to reach and engage with implicit guests. Then is a step-by-step companion on how to effectively announce your Airbnb on social media

1 Identify Your Target followership

Determine the demographics, interests, and actions of your ideal guests.

conform your content to reverberate with your target followership.

2. Choose the Right Social Media Platforms

Select platforms that align with your target followership and property type.

Consider platforms like Instagram, Facebook, Twitter, and Pinterest, which are popular for trip-related content.

3. Optimize Your Social Media Biographies

produce professional and visually appealing biographies on chosen platforms.

Use high-quality images of your Airbnb property as profile and cover prints.

Include a terse and compelling memoir with a call to action.

4. Produce engaging Visual Content

Show your Airbnb with high-quality prints and videos.

Emphasize the unique features, aesthetics, and gests your property offers.

Use professional photography to make a strong first print.

5. Tell a Compelling Story

Craft engaging narratives about your property, original lodestones, and guest gests.

Share behind-the-scenes content to humanize your hosting experience.

6. use stoner- Generated Content

Encourage guests to partake in their guests and tag your Airbnb.

Repost and punctuate stoner-generated content to make a sense of community.

7. Incorporate Hashtags

produce ingrained hashtags for your Airbnb.

Use applicable and trending trip or position-grounded hashtags.

Include a blend of niche and popular hashtags to maximize visibility.

8. unite with Influencers

Identify and reach out to social media influencers in the trip or life niche.

unite on patronized posts or hookups to reach a broader followership.

9. Run Promotional juggernauts

to produce limited-time elevations or abatements.

Host contests or comps to increase engagement and visibility.

10. Optimize for Each Platform

conform your content grounded on each platform's strengths and followership.

Use Instagram for visually appealing prints, Facebook for community engagement, and Twitter for real-time updates.

11. Donated Advertising

Explore paid advertising options on platforms like Facebook and Instagram.

Define your target followership and set a budget to reach a larger followership.

12. Partake Original gests

Highlight near lodestones, caffs, and conditioning.

Showcase your Airbnb as a gateway to a unique trip experience.

13. Respond to commentary and dispatches

Engage with your followership by responding to commentary and dispatches instantly.

Foster a sense of community and responsiveness.

14. Track Analytics and Acclimate Strategies

Use analytics tools on each platform to cover performance.

Acclimate your strategy based on what content resonates most with your followership.

15. thickness is crucial

Maintain a harmonious advertisement schedule to keep your followership engaged.

trial with different advertisement times to identify peak engagement ages.

16. Connect with Original Businesses

and unite with original businesses for cross-promotion.

Share content that emphasizes the original community and culture.

17. Encourage Direct Bookings

Include a direct booking link in your social media biographies.

Encourage followers to bespeak directly through your website for a flawless experience.

By enforcing these strategies, you can effectively announce your Airbnb on social media, adding visibility, attracting eventuality guests, and erecting a strong online presence for your property.

The Power of Original Collaborations: structure Community Connections

- Fit the value of original collaborations in enhancing the overall guest experience.
- Establishing connections with nearby businesses to produce a sense of community.

Relating Implicit Collaborators

Understanding Your Guests' Interests

- relating businesses that align with the interests and preferences of your target guests.
- Considering original lodestones, caffs, tenures, and unique guests.

Original Niche requests

- Exploring niche requests and relating specialty businesses that can add unique value.
- feeding to specific interests, similar to art, adventure, or heartiness.

Casting a Compelling Collaboration Pitch

easily Articulating Benefits

- Outlining the collective benefits of collaboration for both your Airbnb and the original business.

- Emphasizing how collaboration enhances the overall guest experience.

Showcasing Win- Win scripts

- Demonstrating how the collaboration can affect a palm-palm situation for all parties involved.
- pressing implicit business growth and increased visibility.

Types of Collaborations

Cross-Promotions

- Coordinating promotional conditioning with original businesses.
- Offering exclusive abatements or packages for guests who engage with both your Airbnb and the mating business.

common Events

- Hosting common events or conditioning that showcase the unique immolations of both realities.
- uniting on special occasions or themed events.

Original hookups

- Establishing long-term hookups with original businesses.
- Negotiating deals or arrangements that profit both parties over an extended period.

enforcing cooperative Packages

Curated gests

- Designing curated packages that combine the immolations of your Airbnb with those of original businesses.

- Creating themed gests that tell a cohesive story.

Exclusive Abatements

- Negotiating exclusive abatements or gratuities for your Airbnb guests with uniting businesses.
- Enhancing the overall value proposition for guests.

cooperative Marketing sweats

Social Media Cross-Promotion

- uniting on social media juggernauts to cross-promote each other's immolations.
- participating in each other's content to expand reach and engagement.

Coordinated Content Creation

- uniting on content creation, similar to blog posts, vids, or social media stories.
- Showcasing the cooperative sweats and unique guests.

Flawless integration for Guests

Streamlined Guest Experience

- icing a flawless experience for guests when engaging with uniting businesses.
- furnishing clear instructions and information about collaboration immolations.

instructional coffers

- Creating instructional coffers, similar to leaflets or attendants, that highlight original businesses and their collaborations.
- Making these coffers fluently accessible to guests.

Building Long- Term Connections Harmonious Communication

- Maintaining regular communication with uniting businesses.
- Addressing enterprises instantly and fostering positive connections.

Periodic Review and Refinement

- Periodically reviewing the effectiveness of collaborations.
- Refining strategies and exploring new openings for enhancement.

Showcasing Original Culture and Moxie

Authentic Original gests

- uniting with businesses that embody the original culture and spirit.
- furnishing guests with authentic gests that go beyond typical sightseer immolations.

Original Expertise Sessions

- Arranging sessions or shops with original experts to enrich the guest experience.
- Offering perceptivity into the community's history, traditions, or artificer.

Creating a Cooperative Culture

Encouraging Community Engagement

- Encouraging guests to engage with original businesses and partake in their guests.
- Fostering a sense of community and connection.

Community Events

- sharing in or hosting community events that involve uniting businesses.
- Strengthening ties with the original community.

Legal and Logistics Considerations

Clear Agreements

- Establishing clear agreements with uniting businesses.
- Defining terms, liabilities, and prospects.

Legal Compliance

- icing that collaborations cleave to original regulations and legal conditions.
- Seeking legal advice when necessary to navigate any complications.

Nonstop evaluation and adaption

Regular Performance Reviews

- Conducting regular reviews of cooperative sweats.
- Gathering feedback from guests and uniting businesses for nonstop enhancement.

adaption to Market Trends

- Staying informed about request trends and conforming collaborations consequently.
- Exploring new trends and inventions in original businesses and trip gests.

This chapter provides a comprehensive companion on uniting with original businesses to enhance the success of your Airbnb. By erecting strong connections, creating charming packages, and fostering a cooperative culture, you can elevate the guest experience, boost your property's appeal, and contribute appreciatively to the original community. nonstop evaluation and adaption ensure that your collaborations remain applicable and effective over time.

CHAPTER SEVEN
SCALING YOUR AIRBNB BUSINESS
how to Expand Your Property Portfolio on Airbnb

Expanding your property portfolio on Airbnb requires a strategic and methodical approach. In this chapter, we will explore crucial strategies and considerations to help you grow your Airbnb business, acquire new parcels, and maximize your success in the short-term reimbursement request.

Market Analysis and Opportunity Assessment

Market Research: Conduct thorough request exploration to identify areas with high demand for short-term settlements.

dissect trends, original events, and trip patterns to pinpoint economic openings.

Guest Profile Analysis: Understand the demographics and preferences of your target guests in implicit expansion locales.

conform your property selection to feed to the specific requirements of different guest parts.

Financial Planning and Investment

Financial Assessment: estimate your current fiscal standing and establish a budget for property accession.

Explore backing options, similar to mortgages, loans, or hookups.

ROI Analysis: Conduct a comprehensive analysis of implicit Return on Investment (ROI) for new parcels.

Assess the long-term growth eventuality and profitability of prospective investments.

Property Selection Criteria

position Prioritization: Prioritize locales with high sightseer demand, propinquity to lodestones, or arising hotspots.

Consider factors like availability, safety, and original amenities.

Diversification Strategy: Diversify your property portfolio by considering different types and sizes of parcels.

acclimatize to the preferences of your target followership in each unique position.

Network Structure and Assiduity Connections

Forge Local connections: figure connections with original real estate agents, property directors, and assiduity professionals.

influence original perceptivity and moxie to make informed opinions.

Networking Events: Attend real estate and hospitality networking events to establish connections with implicit mates.

Explore collaboration openings with other property possessors or investors.

Addition and Property improvement

Addition Strategy: Consider parcels that may profit from emendations to increase their value.

Budget for advancements and advancements aligned with guest prospects.

Sustainability enterprise: Incorporate sustainable and energy-effective upgrades to appeal to environmentally conscious trippers.

Enhance the overall sustainability of your property portfolio.

Legal Compliance and Regulatory Understanding

Original Regulations Research: Conduct a thorough exploration of original regulations, zoning laws, and licensing conditions.

ensure compliance with legal scores for short-term settlements in each position.

duty Counteraccusations: Understand the duty counteraccusations associated with retaining and renting parcels in different regions.

Consult with duty professionals to optimize your fiscal strategy.

Scalable Operations and Effective operation

Streamlined functional Processes: Develop effective functional processes that can be gauged to manage multiple parcels.

apply centralized operation systems and tools for streamlined operations.

Professional Property Management: Consider hiring professional property directors or exercising property operation services.

Delegate tasks similar to guest communication, cleaning, and conservation for optimal effectiveness.

Strategic Marketing for New Properties

Pre-Launch Marketing: figure expectation for new parcels through-launch marketing juggernauts.

use social media, dispatch newsletters, and your being guest base to produce mindfulness.

harmonious Branding: Maintain harmonious branding across all parcels to enhance recognition.

produce a cohesive narrative that ties together your entire property portfolio.

Guest fidelity Programs Across-Promotions

Multi-Property fidelity impulses: Introduce fidelity programs that award guests for staying across multiple parcels.

Offer exclusive abatements, gratuities, or early booking boons.

Cross-Promotions: Applecross promotions between different parcels in your portfolio.

Encourage guests to explore the variety within your portfolio for a different experience.

Nonstop evaluation and Adaptation

Performance Metrics Tracking: Regularly track performance criteria for each property in your portfolio.

dissect residency rates, guest satisfaction, and fiscal returns.

Feedback Integration: Incorporate guest feedback and reviews to make nonstop advancements.

acclimatize your strategy grounded on evolving guest preferences and request trends.

threat Mitigation Strategies

Diversification of Investments: Diversify your property investments to spread threat across different locales and property types.

Balance high-threat, high-price openings with further stable options.

Comprehensive Insurance: ensure comprehensive insurance content for each property.

alleviate implicit fiscal pitfalls associated with property damage, liability, or unlooked-for events.

Long-Term Vision and Sustainability

Strategic Growth Plan: Develop a long-term vision and growth plan for your property portfolio.

Identify openings for sustainable expansion and request dominance.

Sustainable Practices: Incorporate sustainable practices into your property operation and operations.

Emphasize environmental responsibility and social impact for a flexible business model.

This comprehensive companion provides a roadmap for expanding your property portfolio on Airbnb. By combining request analysis, strategic planning, and a commitment to excellence, you can successfully grow your Airbnb business and subsidize the openings presented by the dynamic short-term reimbursement request.

Hiring Assistance and Outsourcing Tasks for Airbnb Success

As your Airbnb business grows, managing colorful tasks on your own can come inviting. This chapter explores the strategic process of hiring backing and outsourcing tasks to streamline operations, enhance effectiveness, and concentrate on what matters most — furnishing an exceptional guest experience.

Assessing Your requirements

Task Analysis: Conduct a thorough analysis of the tasks involved in managing your Airbnb property.

Identify areas that can profit from external support, similar to cleaning, conservation, or guest communication.

Skill Gap Identification: Assess your chops and determine where you may warrant moxie or time.

Pinpoint tasks that can be better handled by specialists.

Types of Assistance

Cleaning Services: Hire professional cleaning services to ensure your property is constantly well-maintained.

Establish clear guidelines and prospects for drawing staff.

Property Management Companies: Consider outsourcing property operation tasks to a professional company.

use their moxie in guest communication, bookings, and day-to-day operations.

Virtual sidekicks and executive Support

Virtual sidekicks: Hire virtual sidekicks to handle executive tasks, dispatch correspondence, and reserve inquiries.

Free up your time to concentrate on strategic aspects of your Airbnb business.

client Support Services: Explore outsourcing client support to handle guest inquiries and enterprises.

ensure clear communication guidelines are handed to maintain your property's character.

Marketing and Content Creation

Content pens and shutterbugs: Hire professionals for content creation, including writing compelling property descriptions and taking high-quality prints.

Showcase your property effectively to attract further guests.

Social Media directors: Employ social media directors to handle your online presence.

produce engaging content, respond to commentary, and apply strategic marketing juggernauts.

Legal and fiscal Experts

Accountants and Tax Professionals: Seek backing from accountants and duty professionals to manage fiscal aspects.

ensure compliance with duty regulations and optimize your fiscal strategy.

Legal Consultants: Consider consulting with legal professionals to navigate original regulations and contractual agreements.

cover your business from implicit legal challenges.

Technology and robotization

Property Management Software: Invest in property operation software to automate booking processes and streamline operations.

influence technology to enhance effectiveness and association.

Smart Home Systems: apply smart home systems for crucial entry, security, and energy operations.

Enhance the guest experience while reducing homemade tasks.

Hiring Process

Define places and liabilities: easily define the places and liabilities for each position you plan to fill.

Develop job descriptions outlining prospects and qualifications.

Reclamation Strategies: Use colorful reclamation channels, similar to job boards, professional networks, or referrals.

Conduct thorough interviews to assess campaigners' chops and comity.

Training and Onboarding

Detailed Onboarding Process: Develop a detailed onboarding process for new hires.

give comprehensive training on your property's unique features and service norms.

Communication Protocols: Establish clear communication protocols to ensure effective collaboration.

use tools similar to communication apps and design operation software.

Performance Monitoring and Feedback

crucial Performance pointers (KPIs): Define crucial performance pointers applicable to each part.

Regularly cover KPIs to estimate the performance of your platoon.

Feedback Channels: Establish open feedback channels for nonstop enhancement.

Encourage platoon members to give perceptivity on process advancements.

Cost-Benefit Analysis

Estimate Cost Savings: Conduct a cost-benefit analysis to determine the fiscal impact of outsourcing tasks.

Assess the overall value added to your business.

Inflexibility and Scalability: Consider the inflexibility and scalability of outsourced services.

ensure that external support can acclimatize to the evolving requirements of your Airbnb business.

Maintaining a particular Touch

Guest Communication Guidelines: easily communicate your prospects for guest communication to your platoon.

Maintain a substantiated touch to enhance the guest experience.

Regular Check- sways: Schedule regular checks- sways with your platoon to foster a sense of connection.

ensure that everyone is aligned with your property's pretensions and norms.

Legal and Ethical Considerations

Contractual Agreements: Establish clear contractual agreements with outsourced service providers.

Define prospects, deliverables, and confidentiality clauses.

Ethical Practices: ensure that outsourced services align with ethical business practices.

Choose mates who partake in your commitment to quality and integrity.

nonstop enhancement

Feedback Loops: Establish feedback circles to gather perceptivity from both guests and platoon members.

Use feedback to identify areas for enhancement and invention.

adaption to Changing Needs: Stay nimble and adaptable to changing request trends and guest preferences.

Modify your outsourcing strategy to align with evolving business demands. Hiring backing and outsourcing tasks are integral ways of optimizing your Airbnb business for growth and effectiveness. By strategically relating your requirements, embracing external support, and maintaining a balance between robotization and personalization, you can elevate your property operation and concentrate on furnishing an outstanding experience for your guests.

CHAPTER EIGHT
CASE STUDIES AND SUCCESS STORIES ON AIRBNB
Unveiling the Secrets of Airbnb Triumph

This chapter delves into real-world exemplifications of Airbnb hosts who haven't only navigated challenges but also achieved remarkable success. By exploring these case studies, you will gain perceptivity into the strategies, inventions, and unique approaches that set these hosts piecemeal in the dynamic world of short-term settlements.

Case Study 1 The Art of Niche Hosting

Background

Host Profile: Jane Turner is an artist and Airbnb host.

Niche Focus: Creating an art-themed Airbnb experience.

Strategies and Success Factors

Immersive Art Experience: Jane converted her property into an immersive art gallery, showcasing her work and that of original artists.

Collaborations: Partnered with original art seminaries and workrooms, hosting art classes and shops for guests.

Guest Engagement: Encouraged guests to produce their art, fostering a unique and memorable experience.

Case Study 2 Sustainable Stays

Background

Host Profile: Alex and Sarah Green, are eco-conscious Airbnb hosts.

Niche Focus: furnishing sustainable and eco-friendly accommodation.

Strategies and Success Factors

Herbage enterprise: enforced eco-friendly practices similar to solar panels, rainwater harvesting, and energy-effective appliances.

Educational Outreach: handed information to guests about sustainable living and encouraged responsible tourism.

Positive Reviews and Recognition: entered accolades for their commitment to sustainability, attracting like-inclined guests.

Case Study 3 The Multi-Property Maven

Background

Host Profile: Michael Nguyen is a successful multi-property Airbnb host.

Niche Focus: Strategic accession and operation of multiple parcels.

Strategies and Success Factors

Request Analysis: Conducted thorough request exploration to identify high-demand locales.

Effective Operations: enforced streamlined functional processes and outsourced tasks to professional property directors.

Brand thickness: Maintained harmonious branding across all parcels, fostering guest fidelity.

Case Study 4 Transformative Technology Relinquishment

Background

Host Profile: Emily Rodriguez, tech-smart Airbnb entrepreneur.

Niche Focus: using technology for an enhanced guest experience.

Strategies and Success Factors

Smart Home Integration: enforced crucial entry, automated check-heft, and smart home features.

Virtual Concierge: employed AI-driven virtual sidekicks for guest communication and original recommendations.

Positive Reviews and Referrals: Garnered positive reviews for the flawless and tech-forward experience, leading to increased bookings.

Case Study 5 Community-Centric Hosting

Background

Host Profile: Javier and Maria Gonzalez host with a community focus.

Niche Focus: Creating a sense of community for guests.

Strategies and Success Factors

Original hookups: Banded with nearby businesses, offering exclusive abatements to guests.

Community Events: Hosted regular events, similar to neighborhood tenures, cooking classes, and artistic gatherings.

Guest fidelity Programs: enforced fidelity impulses, encouraging reprise bookings and referrals.

Case Study 6 The revivification design

Background

Host Profile: Tom and Lisa Thompson host with a passion for major parcels.

Niche Focus: Renovating and revitalizing major homes.

Strategies and Success Factors

Property Transformation: repaired literal parcels, conserving architectural charm while adding ultramodern amenities.

Storytelling: Shared the history of each property, creating a narrative that reverberated with guests.

Media Coverage: entered media attention for their restoration systems, attracting niche followership. These case studies illustrate the diversity of success stories within the Airbnb community. Whether through niche hosting, sustainability, technology integration, community engagement, or major property restoration, these hosts showcase the creativity and invention that contribute to Airbnb's triumphs. By learning from these exemplifications, you can draw alleviation to shape your unique path to success in the dynamic world of short-term settlements.

CHAPTER NINE

THE RESOURCES AND TOOLS FOR AIRBNB HOSTS

Elevate Your Airbnb Hosting Game

In the competitive geography of short- term settlements, arming yourself with the right coffers and tools can significantly enhance your effectiveness, guest experience, and overall success as an Airbnb host. This chapter explores a comprehensive list of coffers and tools designed to empower hosts and streamline colorful aspects of property operation.

Property operation Platforms

Airbnb Host Dashboard

Purpose: Centralized platform for managing bookings, communication, and property details.

crucial Features: reserving operation, guest messaging, and timetable synchronization.

Guesty

Purpose: Comprehensive property operation platform for Airbnb hosts.

crucial Features: robotization of guest communication, task operation, and channel operation.

Dynamic Pricing Tools

Price Labs

Purpose: Dynamic pricing optimization for maximizing profit.

crucial Features: Automated pricing adaptations grounded on request demand, contender analysis, and seasonality.

Beyond Pricing

Purpose: AI- driven dynamic pricing for Airbnb rosters.

crucial Features: Real- time price adaptations, request trend analysis, and profit maximization.

drawing and conservation Services

Handy

Purpose: On- demand cleaning and conservation services.

crucial Features: drawing, repairs, and conservation tasks listed to align with guest successions.

duly

Purpose: Property medication and task operation.

crucial Features: rosters for drawing and property setup, icing thickness.

Virtual Adjunct and robotization Tools

My BnB Assistant

Purpose: Virtual adjunct for automated guest communication.

crucial Features: Automated messaging, check- in instructions, and custom guest relations.

Smartbnb

Purpose: AI- driven guest communication and robotization.

crucial Features: Automated messaging, inquiry responses, and substantiated guest gests.

Legal and Regulatory Assistance

Lodge Link

Purpose: Legal compliance and nonsupervisory support.

crucial Features: Stay informed about original regulations, duty scores, and legal conditions.

Nolo

Purpose: Legal coffers and guidance for property possessors.

crucial Features: papers, attendants, and legal advice on property operation and rental laws.

Financial Management Tools

QuickBooks

Purpose: Account and fiscal operation software.

crucial Features: expenditure shadowing, income reporting, and duty medication.

Host Financials

Purpose: fiscal analytics and reporting for Airbnb hosts.

crucial Features: Income and expenditure shadowing, profit analysis, and fiscal perceptivity.

Guest Communication and Experience

Your Welcome

Purpose: In- room tablets for guest communication and original recommendations.

crucial Features: Guest information, check- in instructions, and individualized recommendations.

Hello Here

Purpose: Guest experience and communication platform.

crucial Features: Virtual concierge, automated check- heft, and real- time guest support.

Smart Home and Security Systems

August Smart Lock

Purpose: crucial entry and smart cinch technology.

crucial Features: Remote access control, crucial entry for guests, and exertion shadowing.

Nest

Purpose: Smart home and security bias.

crucial Features: Smart thermostats, bank sensors, and security cameras for enhanced property safety.

Marketing and Promotion Tools

Canva

Purpose: Graphic design platform for creating promotional accoutrements.

crucial Features: Templates for social media posts, leaflets, and promotional images.

Mailchimp

Purpose: Dispatch marketing and communication.

crucial Features: Dispatch juggernauts, newsletters, and guest communication robotization.

Guest Reviews and Feedback

Review Trackers

Purpose: Examiner and manage online reviews.

crucial Features: Review shadowing, sentiment analysis, and character operation.

GuestRevu

Purpose: Guest feedback and character operation.

crucial Features: checks, reviews, and practicable perceptivity for perfecting guest satisfaction.

nonstop literacy and Support

Airbnb Community Center

Purpose: Online community for hosts to connect, partake perceptivity, and seek advice.

crucial Features: Forums, conversations, and coffers for hosts at all experience situations.

Airbnb Help Center

Purpose: Comprehensive support and FAQs for hosts.

crucial Features: Attendants, papers, and troubleshooting backing for common issues. Equipping yourself with the right coffers and tools is vital in achieving success as an Airbnb host. Whether you are fastening on property operation, guest experience, legal compliance, or marketing, the different array of tools available can streamline your sweats and elevate your hosting game. Regularly explore new tools and stay streamlined on assiduity trends to ensure your hosting strategy remains innovative and effective.

CONCLUSION

MASTERING THE ART OF AIRBNB BUSINESS

Embarking on the trip of Airbnb hosting is an adventure filled with openings, challenges, and the eventuality of satisfying success. As we conclude this comprehensive companion, it's essential to reflect on the crucial takeaways and perceptivity that can guide you in learning the art of the Airbnb business.

- ## Embrace nonstop literacy

The Airbnb geography is dynamic and ever-evolving. Success as a host requires a commitment to nonstop literacy. Stay informed about assiduity trends, guest preferences, and changes in regulations. Engage with the Airbnb community, seek advice, and be open to conforming your strategies grounded on new perceptivity.

- ## Prioritize Guest Experience

At the heart of a thriving Airbnb business is an exceptional guest experience. Prioritize cleanliness, communication, and personalization. Anticipate guest requirements and go the redundant afar to produce a memorable stay. Positive guest reviews not only enhance your property's character but also attract further bookings.

- ## Strategic Property Management

Effective property operation is the foundation of Airbnb's success. influence property operation platforms, dynamic pricing tools, and robotization to streamline operations. Outsourcing tasks similar to drawing and conservation can free up your time, allowing you to concentrate on strategic aspects of your business.

• Navigate Legal and Financial Considerations

Understanding and clinging to original regulations, duty scores, and legal conditions is pivotal. Seek professional advice when demanded to ensure compliance. Keep scrupulous fiscal records, use account tools, and consider the fiscal counteraccusations of your business opinions.

• influence Technology Wisely

Smart home systems, virtual sidekicks, and technology-driven tools can enhance effectiveness and elevate the guest experience. Embrace inventions that align with your hosting pretensions. still, balance technology with a particular touch to maintain a warm and welcoming atmosphere.

• Diversify and Expand Strategically

Consider diversifying your Airbnb portfolio grounded on request openings and guest demand. Strategic expansion requires thorough request exploration, fiscal planning, and a focus on scalable operations. Whether it's acquiring new parcels or exploring niche requests, strategic growth can contribute to long-term success.

• Foster Community Connections

unite with original businesses, engage with the community, and produce a sense of belonging for your guests. Building positive connections can lead to cooperative openings and enhance the overall experience for both hosts and guests.

• Stay flexible and Adaptive

The Airbnb geography, like any business terrain, can present challenges. Stay flexible in the face of lapses and view challenges as openings for growth. Continuously acclimatize your strategies, learn from guests, and upgrade your approach grounded on feedback and perceptivity. In the realm of Airbnb hosting, success isn't just about furnishing a place to stay but creating a home down from home for your guests. It's about casting unique guests, embracing invention, and navigating the complications of property operation. By combining business wit with a genuine passion for hospitality, you have the eventuality to not only thrive in the Airbnb ecosystem but also leave a continuing impact on the trippers who choose to stay with you.

As you embark on or continue your Airbnb trip, flashback that learning the art of the Airbnb business is an ongoing process. Stay married to excellence, continuously evolve, and delight your guests with unequaled hospitality. May your Airbnb business be a source of both particular fulfillment and professional success. Happy hosting